Hymnody of the Blue Heron

Hymnody of the Blue Heron

Poems by Kevin E. Hadduck

Cherry Grove Collections

Published by Cherry Grove Collections
P.O. Box 541106
Cincinnati, OH 45254-1106

ISBN: 9781625491800

Poetry Editor: Kevin Walzer
Business Editor: Lori Jareo

Visit us on the web at http://www.cherry-grove.com/

Dedication

Linda, you've read every poem I've ever written as an adult, multiple times, despite not caring much for poetry. You've been among my keenest readers, despite finding poetry so often abstruse. And you've seen to the journal publication of most of my poems; I otherwise would not likely have published even one. Without your dedication, I would not be writing this dedication. Let me be clear: this book is yours.

Acknowledgements

I owe a deep debt of gratitude to a number of friends.

Thank you Linda Skiles-Hadduck for your encouragement, wisdom, inspiration, and unflinchingly honest critiques through nearly 36 years together.

Thank you Jay Bouchard for providing me with so much enthusiastic help in assembling this book and for researching and communicating with publishers over the past two years.

Thank you Bill Sroufe for several years of generative conversations about poetry and for insightful scanning and commentary.

Thank you Dr. James Barcus and Dr. James LeMaster for many years of wisdom, instruction, and encouragement.

Thank you Laura Ingram, Lorne Mook, and Charles Beach for your insightful readings.

Thank you to the many kind journal editors who have found my work worthy of publication, and especially to those editors who have taken the time to comment, even on poems they rejected.

Thank you family and friends who have read my poetry, often sent to you unsolicited, and sent encouraging words, or at least smiles, in return. All of you, those I've named and many more, have been a source of inspiration and insight, such that my best poetic efforts merely give back to you what you gave to me. Friendship is a deep well, fed by love from those who drink of it.

Grateful acknowledgement is also made to the journals where these poems first appeared.

The Anglican Catholic: Will Gravity Defy My Praise?

Anglican Theological Review: More

The Appalachian Journal: A Meditation at Half-life, Bristol, Tennessee

Bellowing Ark:
    A Fishing Song for my Wife
    Above the Autumn Moon
    Alleluias of the Red Tail
    By April Moons
    Dancer
    Downwind of the Butterfly
    Hymnody of the Blue Heron
    Meditations on Marie

The Christian Century:
    Breathe into this Body
    Fossil
    Handwriting

Cottonwood: In a Small Café

Country Connections: Ritual

Journal of the American Medical Association:
    A Note to His Doctor
    Father, Though I Am Strong
    Guilt: A Chapter in the History of Pop Psychology
    Hope
    To a Friend in the Ward

Waving Man, 5th Street and I-35, Waco

Literature and Belief: The Day Becomes Cathedral

Lullwater Review:
      Killer Tornado Hits Haven
      You Know What I've Been *Plainsongs:*
      A Taste of Self Pity
      Among Trees
      Heron
      Hunger Drives the Crescent Swallow's Wings
      If Love were Poetry
      Tree Down in a Flat Field
      Under the Pure Sun

Presbyterian Record: Toward Autumn, Buxom and Ripe

Radix: Nocturne

The Rolling Coulter: We Are Going Away

Sisters Today: Advice Out of Season

Sojourners:
      Firethorn
      What I have Seen

South Dakota Review:
      Dark Proverbs
      I will Look for You, Although
      Images from the Cemetery, Kansas and Nebraska
      Pheasant in the Corn

Theology Today:
      A.M.
      Signpost

The Heavens Measure Carnage

The Wisconsin Review: For my Sister Dying

Table of Contents

I Will Look for You, Although

in a wheel rut, where tires stir the melting snow,
the form of a bird disappears.

Flocks of blackbirds and starlings and sparrows
do not pause at its grave.

Feathers and bones lie askew, and rags of skin,
food for the ravening spring.

This bird will not rise like sprout from seed.
The ants digest its memory.

The buds do not remember the flowers, and I see
nothing here in this mud,

and nothing among the chill branches of April to prove,
my friend, that we will meet again.

Heron

It stands hieroglyphic against the reeds.
If it does not move, you will not see
the odd angle of the tucked leg.
Only the delicate fray of feathers
along its neck shifts with the cat-tails.

The mud along the bank keeps no record
of it thrashing, pulling away toward water,
feeling the teeth crushing its leg bone,
the claws grasping at its wing or parrying
the thrust of its long and frantic beak.

Still, the marsh waters leach the fallen leaves
and hide as well the darting bass and bluegill.
Roots of willow twine with muskrat bones.
Paired stilts and coupled bitterns weave,
while bobcats and horned owl wake to ravel.

For now, healing, the heron waits—mock stoic
in a lacework of plum thicket and goldenrod—
for a necessary shad or a crawfish scrambling.
The heron dips, then tips its head to swallow,
its motion, a brief hiatus in the frieze.

A.M.

In that long hour,
from rubbing my eyes
at light pushing through curtains
to stretching on the first sock—
In that long hour
before the mundane day
takes me to task—
In that long hour
passing quickly as it does,
as the egg sizzles
and the *Times* lies waiting—
In that long hour
of slow rising,
the mind asks,
bold in its cover of fog,

Has all been done well?
Have my years made a story?
Do my days scan
and hours parse
and minutes connote
like fine diction?

Outside, a dog's bark
mixes with traffic,
a door slams,
a small plane crosses
the forgetful sky.

Among Trees

Among trees and without
the indifference of a cat,
I am envious.

I feel the same air, the same rain,
the same drying of the sun,

but I do not green with sunlight,
do not feel the slow surge of water
through the soles of my feet.

I am not the earth's
as trees are the earth's,
and the sky is an absence,
the stars too distant
for wings or for relevance,

except
I see the prodigal evening sun
flame among the leaves
its lavender and orange.

Killer Tornado Hits Haven

Last night, stumbling among words
Like a child among heavy tools,
A reporter at the scene said,
"A killer tornado, one mile in diameter,
Cut a swath three blocks wide through Haven."
One woman, hands balled up into fists,
Kept trying to speak. Another smiled,
Shook her head, and walked away shrugging.

This year, as every, someone will win
An award for journalism or poetry
Or some feat involving the adroit use
Of language: "He who most adeptly
Pinned the label 'cow' or 'beef'
On the rump of the bull that just passed
Through a china shop." Meanwhile,
The thing itself, all muscle and bone
And hot breath, goes on stampeding.

Alleluias of the Red Tail

Drive, fleck-breasted bullet, down.
Plummet, plunge, pierce-eyed plume.
Test the aim of talons, bow-string taut.

Lay siege my word-lack, lackluster
Language, razor-wing; rend wide
The curtain-sky, slice cloud-veils.

Pounce, grasp mouse and mole, rapt,
Fear-stunned, mumbling close among
Furrowed wheat and fallow. Rise, raise

Me, mouse, groundling, in your gullet,
Dying at your every word-wing beat.
In fire-hunger, aery alchemist, consume.

In the heat of heart-blood, I, convert,
Will become body, embodied, bidden
Voice, your throat's cry, here to hail,

Call, declare you, your dominion,
Draw into chorusing your choirs,
Singing, winging your alleluias.

More

The young lover asks,
"Why do you still bring me flowers?"
"I am wooing you," replies the Friend.

The eternal pose of Love is wooing.
The constant stirring in Love is longing.

Our bellies are full. We are content;
yet we stand with mouths open,
crying, "More!"

Beneath Live Oaks

As a mockingbird calls up the sun,
Ruth collects her aloe and sings.
I swing the wood and iron gate,
then step along the stone path
threading hyacinths and cedars.
Wheelbarrow, sand, cement, and rocks
await the scrub of brush and water.
"Good morning, Ruth.
I saw your friend walking a ways back.
He was singing—and staggering."
"When he comes," she said, "let him in."

Ruth watches as I hoist a stone in place.
My miscalculations catch her eye.
She sends me to the pile again.
Lifting another, I look for her nod.
She turns her gaze to desert quail
cutting capers in the grass
and lifts one corner of her mouth:
"Didn't we agree the grain of malachite
highlights best against the quartz?
Try that one, there, near the corner.
Texture is everything in low light."

Leaning on her backyard gate,
Harold serenades her face, her hands,
the moon, as quail dip and cluck and bob
along the garden wall. Ruth waits,
while Harold bells his overture,
entreats her pity for a life misplaced.
She trips the latch and holds her elbow out.
 "You and I, Harold, have been

friends for years. Come in and talk.
We'll see if wind from mountain
live-oaks sends a friendly muse."

Passing by a Bird

On the way to my house,
I see an Eastern Kingbird
perched on my fence, singing.
It reaches its beak down
to stroke the edge of its wing.
Then, as I pass, it looks at me.

I have it all wrong, I think.

A bird, gray and white,
perches on a fence, singing.
It preens a wing-feather
with its beak, then looks up.

And yet,

I move
within the scope of its eyes.
The fence is mine.
I am grateful that the Kingbird
sings on my fence, even if
I cannot sing with him.

Sentence Fragments

Along the creek's floor, trees
Standing or strewn like battle-fallen
Against the banks, their leaves,
A blood-carpet, and we, striding
Like child priests in cathedral afternoons
Of light, of green, gold, and red
Casting shadows of mysterium
Among altar stones—
The raven's harraw, heron's harraaahnk
Trumpetings enough, and cardinal's
Trilling bells enough to accompany
Our naive yet deliberate progress—

In that light, as if we'd fought as we might
Against a jabberwock, against hordes
Of shadow-beasts with flaming eyes—
In that place, yet innocent of blood
And fear, as if we'd braved a hell
To spare the rabbits and the robins,
The shy coons, or the muskrats whom
We ruled without decree or possession,
Who did only as they knew, and lived—
If we had been content thus for all time
To be their observing administrators—

Now we, saddened at our progress,
Interrupted, staggered and staggering,
After years, after days and hours
Of remembering with a clarity of vision
Startled by things gone wrong,
Imprisoned by the sins of our grandfathers,
Snared in conflicts with our fathers,
Hooked and netted by sins of our own,
Unliberated yet from the fragments

Of our sentences remaining unserved,
Remembering—

A young man walking, and in walking,
Emergent as if from a dream, awakening—
Who, searching for the right effect,
Grasping for the righteous affect
Of his becoming and of his cause—

And stepping, each generation of him,
Into what Frontier epic of Freedom,
Expansion, and Empire accomplished,
Along what labyrinth of clover-leafs,
Beneath what profusion of billboards,
What montage of storefront signs
Leading all to his belly or groin,
His whole earth compressed
By internet to ad space, an empire
Of capital promising and promising—

And having searched in vain
For some new West, beyond
His father's fathers' deep-cut trail,
With no bones of bison, grizzly,
Or elk littering the plains and passes,
No sad relics of Iroquois, Comanche,
Blackfoot, or Tlingit strewn underfoot
As evidence of his father's crimes—
Having seen the African blooms
Uprooted, the petals scattered
And still unreconciled—

Stopping short, with no frontier
To cut and blunder through,
No destiny manifesting itself

In open prairie and mountain range,
No Plymouth shores waiting, virginal,
To stab an innocent flag upon—
Grown old in history, therefore,
Before he learned to speak
His own story—

This young man, standing
In a year of thirty-five wars,
Just days beyond the century of war,
Of mass graves and mass weapons
As the pinnacle of our evolution,
Of reefs dead and forests dying,
Memorials to our having lived—
This young man, frenetic, angry
In his new century, his new millennium,
Stepping yet in no direction, waiting
Among the shards of cultures,
Of peoples still drawn by Western lure
And strewn across the world, their faces
Reduced to the simulacra of billboard
And the plastic detritus of gift shop,
Their voices lost in the noise of internet,
The static of relentless television—

This young man, still hearing the call
To serve, to save everything,
At the cusp of too late for anything,
Stepping again, though warily,
As if entering once more a forest
Along the creek's bank, but littered
Now with generations of bald tires
And mud-choked washing machines
Dating back, model after model,
Recounting the whole history of machine,
The creek floor papered in old fliers,

Placards and handbills of defunct regimes—

He, alert but waiting, hearing as well
The familiar harroon of blue heron,
Herald of hope yet lingering
Among reeds, in the silted stream
And crawdad pools, sullied and shrunken,
Nature, yet asserting herself, wooing
And ravishing him with glimpses
Of Eden, while crying for her redemption—

If we should ask now who
Will lead him to the right effect,
Will stand as the righteous affect
Of his becoming and of his cause,
Will liberate him from the fragments
Of his sentence and speak his life
to a point—
And if he, himself the monstrance,
Yet hungering for the host, called out,
Asking where you were, Jesus the Christ,
Recreator of every old thing and new,
And you answered—
Then—

For My Sister Dying

in the off moments
between telephone calls and students
fretting at my desk

even in those brief instants
windows, a door opening
between key strokes

I glimpse, again and again
the weight, the sheer volume
of your grief

this work I flee to
I force my hands to
is a small room

a cabin on the beach; it is dark
the windows open on the ocean
salt spray reaches even to the door

If Love Were Poetry

Last night, over the cliche' of campfire
Warming cliches' of shoreline
And lake surface
Without ripple disturbing the sameness,

The moon duplicated precisely itself
Among redundant hills
And cattail clones.
Geese, in yearly circuit, came and went.

We could long ago have grown bored
With the moon, a persistent cliche'.
We both know
The lunacy of constancy.

I suppose we could both be gone
In search of a new form
And a new light,
As every evening, a day's work done,

You re-appear. Your image, though,
Shy or bold, draws my eye
To a mystery,
That a new moon grows full, not old.

Images from the Cemetery, Kansas and Nebraska

I. Somewhere Near Moundridge

a willow tree
a headstone worn by wind and water
a name there, unfamiliar
in our time and to our children—
High grasses rise and fall
among the markers.
Overhead, a mockingbird
seems to be weeping,
imitating the keen of a beloved
who has not come to kneel
in perhaps a hundred years.

II. The Cemetery in Fog at Alma

Nothing discernable
for more than fifty yards—
wet bark fading to gray
stones precisely cut
and lined with spikes of frost
the distinct conversation of geese.
I and my wife stand
at the graves of her parents,
and suddenly
I feel like I am moving
with great speed
into the fog.

III. In the Jennings Exchange

Just over the crest of a hill,

concealed on the west
by windbreak trees and,
on this day, bright
under the sun,
a wrought-iron archway
leads to a small cemetery—
maybe twenty five or thirty stones
leaning or lying half under the turf.
We bury our telephone cable
along the ditch in front,
but the stones, the names,
seem too far from town,
from anyone's home.

IV. A Few Miles Outside Stanton

The brass marker,
a star of David on its face,
and the dates, April 1-April 4, 1889,
leans slightly, as if reaching,
toward an inside corner of a house.
Families have left it there,
have moved and clipped
around its base,
have passed their deeds on
to newcomers, to strangers.
Often they have stopped
in their work or play
and grown somber by it.

V. Among the Stones at McPherson

A daughter-in-law
and a grandson walk for hours,
reading the map of plots,
studying the lines—

They trace over the lay of stones
again and again, measuring
the spaces between. Finally,
in an empty stretch of grass,
they stop and look up,
their dark faces bright in the sun,
their arms hung now at their sides.
She begins to walk away.
He turns suddenly and scatters
flowers over the wide grass.

VI. At a Low Marker in the Colby Cemetery

A man, not so old, but quiet,
said—and I had asked him nothing—
I come here and look at these dates
and at the cut letters grown indistinct,
the names I know and the names
of those I never knew—
I come here alone to learn what I am,
to know who we are.
Then I walk back into town
for a drink at the Legion hall
with those who will not be much longer.

VII. I Do Not Recall the Where

A tangle of small children,
chasing their wild ball
over the churchyard fence,
run suddenly among graves,
through flowers laid carefully.
They keep laughing,
kicking the ball,
leaping from the stones,
flinging their cut flowers.

Sparrow

The sparrow deftly raises
One gray breast feather
To exorcise, with his beak, a mite.
Then, from his wings, he grooms
A bronze pinion.

Between precise strokes,
He watches, catching snapshots,
Left, right, ahead, behind,
Tilting his head to scan
The sky for silhouettes
Of the hawk, the grass below
For movements of the cat.

He and his fellows will rise
And trouble the hawk,
Driving at its head,
Sweeping courageous arcs
Between its great wings,
Tempting even its talons
With upward lunges at its belly.
They will swoop down
And pester the cat away
From their twittering young.

One or two of them, more,
He himself perhaps, will die
Without care in such escapades.
He will not fear beyond
The quickening of his pulse.
Every tiny rush of air and
Surge of adrenalin celebrates,
Within the watchful eye of God,
The freedom of his own irrelevance

The perseverance of his species,
And the earth's endurance.

Nocturne

Forgiveness comes
(a beast?) to ravish
with its claw. I hear it
fingering the boards.
If I stir, it will rend
my shanty walls,
spring and tear the heaviness
of my heart, and my heart.
Such small power to expose
these my heart's cankers,
these bones burning
like a furnace.
What, though, but a God
could rip me so,
to the marrow,
joint from joint,
and leave me,
at morning light, light,
so much lighter

A Note to His Doctor

My friend, old and passing, said,
"There is more to life than staying alive.
Don't rescue me too much."

On his farm, twelve miles out
by rough gravel roads, he is done
with plowing, spraying, harvesting.
But he is not done watching the sun
sink below the windbreak or listening
to the nighthawks above his fields.
Don't make him move to town.
There is more to tragedy
than dying.

Remembrance

This morning I thought of you,
as a mockingbird stretched
its throat to sing love
for the cardinal, the wren,
the robin. Even the raven heard,
like soundings of his finest thoughts,
rasps and rattlings he found
beautiful. No mere mimicry.

Last night, I awoke to your voice.
Only the mockingbird had spoken,
emptying itself again and again
into the near darkness, hiding
in the shadows of some tree,
its song like moonlight spilling
across the hedgerows.
No mockery in this bright aria.

Today, I will again hear suddenly,
and the mockingbird will dance
in the forsythia, self-possessed
small shadow at the heart
of candle flame, clown and connoisseur
of everybody's tune, every song
its own best. No thievery here.
It is itself your self singing.

This Is Not Enough

This is our Sunday morning
rendezvous among the pillows,
early serenade of predawn voices.
Our torsos rise and fall, curved
and arched, antiphonal, as if
in prayer and exaltation, that
and that indeed. And then
you stand beside the mirror,
my left hand lightly cupping you.
My right hand slips your dress
across your shoulder, tracing
down the sweep of your neck,
the silver chain, the pendant gem.

Why, then, if that were satisfying,
do we dress and search for more
among the dog-eared psalter,
candle-lighted altar, and crucifix?
When morning sun-glow brights
your hair and warms your cheek,
we find our way beneath a cold
cathedral ceiling, singing, bending
bodies, cupped around intangibles
as if we each were lovers. We are
here again for that, and that indeed,
antiphonal in prayer and exaltation.

Again the sun will rise, epiphany
of itself, as if without interpreter,
no need for homily or choir,
waxing eloquent at first in frost
and then, its own oracle, in dew
as glints of joy on Augustine.
This moment, argentine and jeweled,

will once again assert its fire
among the remnant browns and rusts
of late hanging ash and pin oak.

Such brillianting, as presage of
a sudden zeal to copulate, will satisfy,
until it pierces through the mind,
draws up a deeper, keener appetite
to sacrifice a bullock or a dove,
to score the knees on graveled miles,
to search for what anticipates the dew
and keeps it hanging in the heart,
as covenant against an ancient sacrilege,
hope glistening against the dead leaf,
now dry and soon to drop.

That old zeal is not enough,
nor the spring's renascent feathers,
neon among neon buds and sprouts,
nor all the heart's yearnings or fears,
if brown leaves that hang are dead,
if all things that are dead are dead.
What rises then from fecund rot
has no memory, no joy beyond
the moment of its glory. There is
no tragedy, then, if the whole—you,
the sun, the pin oak, the old sacrilege—
in cosmic hiccup, sucks back into itself,
holds captive there all light in stone.

Who will derive from that goodbye
a song? Who will devise a dance
for that farewell, when sunless stone
remains, immense, singular, alone?
There must be span enough, lover,
from fingertip to breastbone, depth

enough from breast to heart's core
to embrace the grandest question,
foil wide enough to cradle the bright
unbounded, the radiant galaxies.

I was not, could not be enough,
even had I muscles drawn in close
embrace, as if a perfect warrior king
with empress, on an antique vase.
You stood, lover, your hair draped
like a sleeping body down your back,
one strand flung like an arm across
your shoulder, and then, that sudden
zeal, deceptive in itself, awakened,
a tremulous and naked question
to an ancient answer, a darker mystery,
a greater light that will suffice.

You Hold a Picture

In one hand, you hold a picture, a lover, and
from your window, you see all of this:

At several miles, high-shouldered
clouds advance, brillianting,
exuberant, heralding
a thrash of branches
and a sudden roar
in the canopy.

Here,
a quivering of light
at the topmost leaflet's edge
ruptures the pale parchment sky,
while house finch and sparrow dart
boldly yet among the hanging feeders.

With fingers of the other hand, you trace
across your brow the lines of fear and resolve.

Ritual

Tonight, on my way home—
the town glowing beyond the horizon
with long stretches of highway
and bridges rushing toward me from
the absolute black of middle distance—
I decided again
not to die
and

tonight, our home still miles away—
with you awaiting me there
your legs stretched along the sofa
your head at rest on one arm
fingers slowly toying with one curl—
I decided again
to live

Why should it surprise you
that often thus, I fold down
the layers of my mind
and drift among dreams
dark and bright, unafraid
to rise again and make up
my mind

that has not once
changed.

Signpost

Like everyone who walks
In the dark along a low road
Leading into town, he comes
To a crossing and no moon
No star shows him where to go

So he stands like a signpost
With no words no direction
No pillar of smoke for guide
No bold woman competing
With monotonous harlots
No one-in-a-thousand preacher
Calling 'young man come away'
No stones whispering
A prelude to his praise

So he stands at two roads
Hoping for a revelation
And knowing this
If he could justify one step
And all the alterations of the world
That step would bring
He could explain the intersection
Of Heaven and Earth and the why
Of a body hung on a crossing
Of two timbers at the end of all roads
Leading to Jerusalem

So he stands like a signpost
At the meeting of two roads

To a Friend in the Ward

On a slope of tundra high above San Luis,
a scar from twenty years ago still writhes
among the rocks where marmots scream.
In another year or so, fine grasses
and flowers small as suture knots
may finally close this shallow cut.
I am amazed at such a surgery,
at the speed of nature's repairs.

They let you go with us for an afternoon.
We watched you shuffle through the park,
saw you make a slow turn at the waist
when a mockingbird took up his drill.
You walked with your arms hung
straight at your side, your ashen face
forward. You were far from there.
Your wounds, festering for thirty years,
have now begun consuming you.

Still, I am amazed by healings
when they come, at the shock they give
my disbelief. Their movement stirs me,
these god-like transmutations
of glacial ice into warm seas.

A Bluegill in a Blue Heron

In this
unlikely composition
of salt marsh
and evening sun

of green walls
gray floor
orange and lavender
ceiling

a porcelain egret
an ebony ibis
a velvet cardinal
hold their perfect poise

while
a bluegill dies

in a blue heron

Crocus

Every year these foolish flowers
punched their colors through snow.
But one year, early, much too early,
a single flower shoved its purple head
up toward a bright hole in the clouds
and spread its leaves, a bold green
against a vacant white.

Our mother saw it first and called.
Running barefoot through the door,
we stepped into the cold to watch,
shivering, a crocus showing off.

Within an hour, a wet snowfall
took the impetuous flower down.

Toward Autumn, Buxom and Ripe

On the window sill again this year,
Poinsettia bones still dangle rags
And drop them one by one into the soil.

Outside, the garden skeletons lie in heaps,
Like fragments rummaged in a plundered dig,
Though greening sprouts will waken soon enough.

Who, six months from now, will split this melon,
Expose its pith and hollowed heart, and say
With greater certainty than fact allows,

The cycles will not end in Winter's pale,
That springs and summers both will pass
And leave us with an Autumn, buxom, ripe,

Unfading?

Forgiveness Begins in Snow

A snowfall lays its delicate shroud
across a crumpled head and breast,
the wings spread as if still fighting
to out-pace a sudden rush of lights.
Not too far away, a small knot of fur
rests mid-road until it too lies buried.

Children, their rude boots pushing
through this fragile winding sheet,
come kicking up the torn remains
of autumn's failures, as if the rains
will not soon bare a confessional
of bone shards, moldered leaves,
and mud, where greening shoots
will rise to a fresh look at the world.

Generations

millennia upon century upon year upon day,
generations of clamant Canada, Snow
and White-Front, of bugling Heron,
Sandhill and Whooper, humming Pelican,
whistling Pintail, Teal and Wood,
of hoarse Shoveler, hooting Canvasback,
laughing Mallard and the shy Bufflehead,
of clucking Coot, grunting Cormorant
and giggling Grebe, of low croaking Egret
and their moaning shadow the ebony Ibis,
of begging Tern and squabbling Gull,
of resonant Bittern and raucous Cowbird,
Starling, Blackbird and Crow
beyond reckoning, of trilling Junco,
sputtering Hummingbird, ringing Sandpipers
and the Plover whistling and growling, all

all shoulder their unintending purposes
down their thousand-mile corridors
from canada to mexico and the islands,
settling their voices into our yards,
along our walks and onto our fields,
counseling in their high rookeries,
contending in their great parliaments
upon the waters and the reeds
of their rivers, marshes, and lakes,
shouting ecstatic as one voice
in their vast congregations

they drop their fertile feces into our parks,
where we power-hose the nuisance away
from our sidewalks and curse their numbers,
and we in our manifest confusions toil
and scream down runways, bear our spoils

50

along rails and canals, our engines howling,
wheels whining with insatiable spin
on highways aimed at irresistible progress
and the securities of perdurable empire
beneath the foreign visages scarred
into a sacred mountain in dakota,
the sioux still dream, and in idaho
the shoshone dream fruitless dreams,
forgetting the hardest thing
for conquered people to remember:
to God, the nations are dust,
yet not one Sparrow falls God-forgotten

and the ageless Pigeons in time square,
the bobble-head Pigeons inelegant on
the eifel, fearless on the tower of london,
Pigeons that do not defer to power
on the onion domes of red square
or across the vacancies of tiananmen,
Pigeons that plaster the golden gate,
ubiquitous clucking Pigeons, pecking
at seeds in our cracked sidewalks,
keep doing what they do without rancor
guile or humor, patiently to our cars,
our windows, our walls, our white houses,
and, yes, to our finest granite noses.

Words Are Not Enough

I want to tell you something, love,
Woven with leaves and branches,
Moonlight shifting on St. Augustine,
And the timbre of a night bird on wind.

Nightsongs among sycamores
And pale light patterned on grass
remind me of love. I cannot explain
Those connections to myself or to you.

I discuss with poets and students,
In iterations on a theme, the medium
Wherein the purling whip-poor-wills
And the peeling sycamores grow distant.

Love, I want to speak in tangibles
About moonlight dancing among leaves.
If I speak with words made of things,
Will you swoon and fall into my arms?

Pheasant in the Corn

Early autumn and the rows of seven-foot corn
Still flaunting their green at the sun, we stood
Beneath in mottled light among the leaves and stalks,
On furrowed dirt, in shadowings of cool.
We could have stayed like that, embraced, the tasseled ear
Stripped bare, the juice of kernels dripping from our chins—
A paradise of soil—and run and rolled, and glimpsed
Occasional blue above our heads if we had cared.
But the chartreuse borer and the steel-toothed fork devour.

late fall
         and snow crust on snow powder
      and wind charging over the rigid furrows
stalks cut short   most lying over
      a few pennants yet
waving tan and gray   tattered glory,   we stood
    shot straight through with the freezing roar of air
   gloved hands deep in pockets   squinting at the blast
of light that hung   frozen   unshadowing
everything   like a tyranny of grace   we might
      have stood like that forever   beautiful as clear
ice
         but the green sprout   conquers.

All season long, the pheasant darts between and down
The rows, in sight—then gone; in view again, but silent—
We have sidelong broken   reckless paths
pursuing him through paradise   of green and
crushed   the burrowed mouse   in snow.
Now we stand   among the corn,   having run

53

reckless and   stopped for breath,   forgetful,
and there he is,   his glance
                     an infinity

Hard Driving Grief Like Pelting Rain

If I groveled in a pasture, grunted through
My gnarled beard and gnawed the grass
On callused hands and knees, would you

Believe I'd sorrowed long enough,
Left villainy behind, or should I die,
Outright, like a criminal hanged?

Then, if I could leap whole-bodied
From a grave, would you forgive,
Or would you probe with fingers first

For scars to keep my memory sharp?
Forgive my fit of arrogance. I'll not
Forget: I was the churning cloud that dealt

Hard driving grief like pelting rain.

Meditations on Marie

She stands in general sun,
But light of her specific face
Is grace.

One evening under stars
She rose from water like a flame.
My gaze

Would come to rest just where
The streams of moonlight draped her eyes
And thighs.

I love the calm of her words,
But dancings of her tongue tip, chin,
And lips,

And motions of her hands
Have drawn me childlike to her breasts
And rest.

If you should see her wash
And pin a medley of all whites,
You might,

As I have often done,
Believe that gods descend on earth
To serve.

Tree Down in a Flat Field

No one blames the sapling
for its fall, small thing and frail.
A child playing football
does it damage in the spring.
A gust of wind may finish it.

This tree, its girth heroic, lies
collapsed in its own shadow,
arms flung wide and toes up.
Did a storm heave it down?
Was it rotten at the core,
its own self-murdering bulk
bringing it to the ground?

The trees at the field's edge, even
the little ones, the old dead ones,
the rotting ones with hearts gone,
all of them, still stand,
                              but this
this is Kansas, Dorothy, where storms
dance wickedly across the earth.

Under the Pure Sun

Sun-glare leaped green from the hedgerows
and the flag-flutter leaf tips of new corn
and disappeared in the blue-white mottle of sky.

I saw the rat take refuge; I startled it hiss-n-spit out.
The open jaws, the thin trails of saliva driving
backward against the rat's jowl and pink throat—

I was this close, then barely out of the way,
as the staccato punch of shotguns ripped
apart the pile of boards he'd burrowed into.

This was my job under the pure sun,
spotter, pointer, chaser, flush the rats out
into the gun sights and dance away laughing—

all done in a simple economy of good and evil,
of rats pillaging and hiding and defecating
against the backdrop of undulating corn fields.

The small apple and pear orchards rose, vulnerable,
along the western fence, where wind-break pines
and bean fields lay stirring toward the horizon.

The pile of boards was once a home that fell to ruin.
We had no remedy for that.

A Fishing Song for My Wife

The current draws my line through reeds of grass
That bend in clumps like heads in meditation.
I will spin the hours here where vines
And willows weave their tendrils overhead
And make an edge of daylight off the bank.
One year an old man standing near the shore
Told me a river god rolls his dark flanks
Along the channel sides and smiles, and fish
That rise are laughter, sent for drawing
Down to water those who walk in sorrow.
I have come down to the waterside.
I'll toss my baited questions, tease my lures,
And wait for sun to glint from gill-plates heaved
With sensuous bellies out into the day.

Hymnody of the Blue Heron

Shy sentinel, perennial watcher
Of marsh and meadow pond, keeper
Of wetland reeds that bend and bow
In wind, that call and at your coming
Sing, hear now our low leaf-rustle,
Our soft, slow soughing, and come.
Stay, and stand near to us.

Blue-gray ghost gone in the fog,
Wing-fan spanning the height of us,
Blue heron, heralding the spring,
Soft-throating the summer sun,
Summoning the autumn chill,
Chortle the shrill-wind winter.
And stay; stand near to us.

Fleeting shadow among clouds,
Purl down from your peregrine ways.
Leave to falcons their dignitary airs.
Rest, and roost among us, who call
In faint reed choirs and wait, stir us,
Wing-billow, breathing through us.
Draw near, and dance with us.

In a Small Café

In a small café, sounds of a truck passing
Take us away from our stoneware cups.
Against the clarity of window glass I glimpse
The fall and rise of your eyelashes.

In a park, where light and shade spill from a tree,
Dappling us and our bench, you turn and look
Across your shoulder at the geese along the shore.
Curves of your ear and brow gather sudden light.

At the market, I come back to your aisle.
I catch the profile of your lips and chin, your hand
At some unruly hair, hovering near your face.
You are bending to inspect apples.

You wait with me on a corner as the light changes.
Then, in a medley of shoulders and purses and
Wind-tousled heads, I hurry to keep pace with you,
Your quick glance to the left exposing your cheek.

Within the flourishes of our hands and dancings
of our lips, there among the rumpled sheets,
I find you. In the glow of our nightstand clock,
I catch the silhouette of your face, turning.

Downwind of the Butterfly

If a butterfly in Bangkok opens its wings
someone pushing a shopping cart along a Bronx alley
will die
or win the lottery
another goes on pushing

as if nothing happened, as if there were
no sweet and sour consequences
downwind
of myriad
butterflies

With a single stride toward home or away
I create a thousand tiny winds
If I remain still
those thousand
will not blow

"Do," says a teacher

"Don't do," says a teacher

Will I be a winged herald or
Will a million prayers with folded hands
deflect sufficient molecules
to work redemption
in our chaos

Dancer

I have seen you dance too little,
have seen the slow weight of my doubt,
the slow rise of my fork at supper
and the slow turn of my head,
make you slow—

Still, remembrance of your hair
bobbing, sweeping shadows
from your cheek, or touches
of your shoes across the floor—
How can I make these mean?

Today, again—you at the window
in shadow by the sink—
the supper sun flings orange
across the shagbark hickory,
and cumulus clouds blossom
orange. Somewhere between
that unendurable billow-flame
of evening cloud and clatter
of dish on pan, you stand,
embodiment of fire,
waiting—

Something like this,
a drawing down of heaven,
heaven-flung fire, to fire again
the ashen strands that cool
the russet of our hair—

A Taste of Self Pity

On dry days,
water does not pour, not drip
from stones, no matter what the whacking
with a stick that seemed divine enough
just yesterday.

That, my love,
in case you wander
on the same parched ground as I,
was a metaphor for the intransigence
of metaphors,

on dry days.
You are not here, so I seek comfort
on this page; but misery yields
these sour words, like vinegar, just
to mock me.

Firethorn

Over chatter of starlings and grackles,
you hear your father's voice,
confident and constant as bee hum
in the backyard of your thoughts.
Echoing along the bedroom halls
of your memory, his voice lingers.
Even my grandfather, as he lay
dying in his son's spare bed,
still heard his father's intonations.
It does not matter if your father
were sage or simple, puissant or pathetic.
You hear his voice troubling you,
now a low intoning, now a thundering,
challenging you again from distraction.
You hear his voice, until one day,
you realize it is not his and has not been
for a long time. Instead, it is the sound
of your own venting, your pleading,
or perhaps your keening for a voice
you never heard, but imagined
and loved to distraction even in absence.
It is, after all, your own obsessive
dadadadadadadaaa until, finally, you
pull your hands away from your ears
and, as a wren chitters in the firethorn,
hear God speak for the first time.

Love Is a Crazy Old Man

They found him in his underwear
At the front door of the wrong house.
The flashing blue and red of the cruiser
Startled an owl. The silent witness
Lifted into the dark and disappeared
With not so much as a timid who.

The dog next door raised her head,
Let go a tentative bark, then stared
Quizzically at her master. She had
Seen him before in his white boxers,
But even in her befuddledog brain,
She knew the door was wrong,
And she wondered why.

Two lots down, across the street,
A neighbor lightly sleeping awakened.
He could see the old man from his window.
There he was again, in his underwear,
Knocking and calling to her.

It must have been that he rolled over,
Found only her pillow and,
As he had done through the months
Since her passing, went looking for her.

The neighbor thought and then,
Before returning to his bed, surmised
That the old man's life boiled down
To a few indispensable clichés:
He is not sure who he is without her.
He is more faithful than a dog.
He would go out hoping, even
In his underwear, to find her again.

A Meditation at Half-life, Bristol, TN

A headstone marked "Defender of the Bridge"
Catches sunlight, and I, at forty-seven
Touch the granite, lean for a moment
Over the place of his bones and ask him,
"What is my name? Who will I become?
What have I done, and what will I do?"

I imagine a boy, bareback on his small horse,
Throwing his arms in large strokes, then turning
His head to watch where he has just passed.
A girl stands, her fingers raised near her face,
Her hand turning as if in a light wind.
He comes every day, and she watches him.

I imagine an old woman sitting on her porch,
Laying a book in her lap, stroking the arm
Of a chair, empty beside her. Nearby,
Forsythia petals flame their yellow in the sun,
As if blown by the breeze of someone passing,
A boy on his pony, waving in large strokes.

The old woman pauses from her book.
"There went the boy who rode with no hands,"
She says, "and crossed the bridge on the river."
The girl with her hand gathered him to herself.
The woman with her hand remembers his hand.
The forsythia remembers its early fire.

On a Cruise for a Moon Pie

Late, at the convenience store,
the lights making it an island,
I saw into a car parked
at the edge of the lot.

In and out of the shadows,
in and out of the glare
of halogen, a man's face
and hands moved as if
in debate.

Two young men,
strutting by in their leathers,
looked at him and laughed.

In the store near the candy,
a cardboard athlete
sold deodorant aimlessly.

A woman at the pump hurries
fumbling with the hose and nozzle
glancing toward that car
mottled in shadow and light.

In ten minutes, no one
who was there
will be.

On a Day of Hard Wind

Stand between hedge-rows a mile apart,
facing across wheat fields, and listen
toward the windward horizon.

Sight past meandering cottonwoods
along creeks and clustered homesteads,
beyond the gray-violet blur, and hear.

Dust devils rage briefly and die out,
Suggest, then deny, a body for wind.
The air makes its relentless assertion.

Formulate questions if you must:
"Why does it pummel me?" Or,
"What does it want from me?"

Still it blows, answerless, but for
the deafening press, like the vast,
persistent haw and hum of a crowd,

a far-off multitude singing their joyous
allelujahs or keening in the throes
of some unanswerable suffering.

Father, Though I Am Strong

Your hammer caught the edge
Of a nail and then the tip
Of your thumb.
We laughed.
When you lifted the tool again,
Your wound forced a lean
In my direction.
Our skin met.
I thrived on that morsel for a week.
It must have frightened you.
I went hungry
Again.
Though I am strong now
And have since found other food,
I cannot forget the brief taste
Of your weakness
And my need.

Pistolero

He stands, legs wide,
shoulders squared,
balled fists slung at his side
like pistolas ready to fire.
He stands.
His eyes do not turn away.
He does not flinch at the truck
rumbling toward his home,
a barreling bandito,
an outlaw on his appaloosa.
He stands.
The truck growls
and bellows near,
headlights blazing.
He stands.
The truck roars
and lurches past his front yard.
This three-year-old,
sans diaper, holds firm.
Only his head turns,
smooth, steady, sure.
His father, diaper in hand
and breathless at the door,
feels a hollowness in his groin.
Pistolero turns at the waist,
Smiles, then fronts again the street.

What I Have Seen

I have seen that I must
Confess to ignorance

I do not know you, although
I have loved you twenty years

The lifting of your lashes
From your cheek

The drawing back by your hand
A lock of your hair

But fully you? I have not seen you
Except through those windows

The green shades surrounding them
The radiant darkness behind them

Press your fingers
Around my arm again

Let's walk, far, long
Tracking through wilderness

You are world enough to explore
For another twenty hundred years

For an army of scientists
Whom I will not invite

But for me, your husband lover,
For all your friends

A clear night sky tells us

In small script your large mystery

You are a bright ground for play
Even a temple where God walks

I have glimpsed his immensities
There

The Heavens Measure Carnage

Before it lives an hour, night has fallen.
A day breaks before it forms.
The clock's hand strikes each minute
As it passes, while solemn bells
Toll the birthing of each hour.

The heavens measure carnage,
And civilizations past, with all
Their lessons, laws, and liturgies,
Have gone like dust, swept aside
By Time's impatient, violent hand.

If across a table we should touch,
What will it matter? And if,
Upon the grazing of our hands, I say,
"I felt the spark of that, like lightening,
here to here," what will it mean?

Say why, when true lovers die, untimely,
Young, the poet sings their timely story,
The scholar makes a study of the tale.
The saint, distracted from his prayers,
Knows what heaven does not measure

And Time cannot destroy.

Breathe into this Body

See these hands
this skin like flaking paint
and these bones like weakening timbers
exposed to rain and wind?

I hear only a voice
lamenting time or loss, resolving
decay into the order of art—
a mouse among splinters and dust

Where are you, you whom I love?
It is your voice I want to hear
your voice saying
  "We lived there in those hands"—

and beyond what strokes
of brush or pen reclaim
the deepening lines, the toppling walls
your lips saying
  "We still live"—

and beyond the generations of mice
beyond the dust
beyond the voice
adding words to words to words—

you, you breathing
the sudden rush of rain the hosannas of wind
into the dust of this body

You Know What I've Been

I would outstretch myself like a field for wheat.
A glint of gull's wing low in the swale,
the rise of swallows from the hills
shouldering the farmer home
might let you say, "Here
I can plant and grow."

I would lie down like a willow-shaded pond,
and fragments of the moon dancing
where herons dip their spears
and an old man tips his pole
might let you say, "Here
I can drink and sleep."

You know what I've been—a dusty man in jeans
carrying boards to his seventh home.
Our tires have gone bald, whispering
again on unfamiliar streets,
and yet you say, "Anywhere,
I will stay with you."

Above the Autumn Moon

On a bright and clear November mind,
I cannot see our distances.

You who wait, and you who come,
you who stay, and you who've gone,

even you who will to keep
as far away as time allows—

you rise with me above the world
and hover here, cartographers

all tracing lines, conferring names,
spanning continents and seas

no broader than a hand and smooth.
See how planets, moons, and suns,

how galaxies converge and rest,
their trillion miles irrelevant.

We lean into each other, press
our lips and plan our rendezvous—

the feasting there, the drinking and
the dance with arms flung wide—

We've kissed again above the moon,
above the autumn moon, and crushed

our breasts against our bones, and here,
we have flown, we have flown.

Antiphonal

I give you the bright bark of trees, love,
and the hard-edged shadows on red brick,
and the window trim that sings
its antiphonal light back at the sky.

This is the afternoon passing:
the shadow of a branch has leaped
one brick's edge closer

to the white wood.

Hope

Three phone calls:
A farm wife with chest pains
Stealing her breath.
A woman with five children,
Her husband gone with her money.
A man who fears his own mind,
For whom his own thoughts
And hands are strangers.
So here I come,
With a twittering gift from God,
Like a schoolboy
Bringing home a robin
Torn by a cat or passing car.
They act grateful for this,
Put their hands gingerly
To the frail, demanding body,
To the beak constantly open,
The claws grasping at a finger,
The discomposed feathers
Of a small thing always near
Dying. I say to them, "Here,
Feed it with water and bread."

Hand Writing

For years I've watched the swallows purl
Their cursive on the air, and never yet,
In all my hours of reading through their lines,
Have I seen even one wing clip another
Or graze a branch or gable end. Each scribes
Its perfect sentences, then takes its place
Along a wire with all the other muses,
Bobbing and chattering as if they'd tricked
The heavy, footed mortals down below
By writing, with invisible ink, inspired verse.
Today, down a footpath I often take,
The angle of a feather draws my eyes
To the dirt, and there, the form of a small bird,
Its wings and legs and torso curled like bones
Of a frail hand, lies among debris.

Until My Dying Day

Until my dying day I'll say
it was not I. I was not there.
I will not turn that way again
will not go back, will not relive.
Until my dying day I'll not.

Until my dying day I'll say
your eyes were lovely as the moon
and just as false. You did not see
or hear. You did not speak for me.
Until my dying day you'll not.

Until my dying day I will
forgive, yet not recall or call.
And why? We never met or touched.
There was no We. And yes, my friend
Until my dying day there will not be.

By April Moons

I don't know the bird that sings
So slowly by the April moons,
Or why it makes a changeable song
Or if it measures grief or joy.
But I will gladly lie awake
Two hours or more and slur my day
To hear the soft articulate throat
Send beauty, unsolicited,
To those who long for rest, not sleep.

Will Gravity Defy My Praise?

To a small throat pulsing,
even from a hill that rests
in fog across a stream,
an ear turns and a mind
awakens like the day.

And when a slender throat,
throbbing, warms, song courses
like blood through footpaths
and deer trails, out along branches
of oak and juniper, to meld
with the new sun.

So easily, so easily the stones
of an outcropping fuse light with echo.
The glare of granite sings and shouts,
while an awakened mind leans,
as if on its elbow, with questions.

How will this stone heart cry out?
With what light? Will this throat,
loosened by the sun's rise, fling its praise
above the reaching tops of elm?
Hosanna? Hosanna?

Guilt: A Chapter in the History of Pop Psychology

There must be someone
or something else to blame,
if not a god,
then perhaps devils
possessing and driving us.
Maybe the stars, deceptive
in their beauty, incline us.
Maybe our mothers,
or the Mother,
or the vasty dark and deep
under the mind
has done us in,
or synapses and their
sly chemical agents.
Maybe we are all
too lizard-like still,
or one link shy
of a kinder, gentler
genetic chain.

A billion wrongful deaths,
but the soiled blade
has no relevance at the scene.
We are about a different logic:
we read by daylight
our own scored bones,
but we didn't do it.
And god must be gone,
or he would fix us all,
send us to our rooms,
deny us pointy objects,
and explain clearly,

once and for all,
what we should have done
instead.

Along the Santa Fe Rails

Stop for a moment while I kneel
To gather a few more stones. See
If I can arch my arm with force
And aim enough to strike the point
These rails converge—it's the attempt
That matters, and straightness of the throw.
On a good day, the rocks, flying
Smoothly as an insight, fall
Between the steel or hit the berm.
But every day, even on the worst,
Our careless sentences flung wild,
The trains go by and disappear
Beyond the point our stones will drop,
Beyond the point our eyes can reach.
Then we stand, dreaming westward
Of those tracks, those busy stations.
And so we bend, spreading our hands,
To gather a few more stones.

We Are Going Away

We are always going away.
From beds with sterile sheets
Or from upholstered chairs, we
Speed suddenly through quiet noons.
And the visiting hour finds us gone
And the noon meal cools forgotten.

Or on mundane streets we pass
The last sign out of town, and days
And years are highways diminishing
Until the roads end and we stand,
Not alone, but waving ourselves on.
And we are going away still,
Always quickly, always soon—

This, then, is my argument for love,
That we compress the hoped-for years
Into the hour we have and grasp
The arm tightly and press the lips
And speak each other into words
That will remain.

Advice Out of Season

Leave the pruning shears alone.
There will be time for burning limbs and leaves.
Watch through the seasons while willows grow
Disorderly and down onto the lawn—
Bent heavy and beautiful like grief.

Dark Proverbs

I. Do not ask for tenderness

An old human is just a sprout
that endured the night's teeth long enough
to be by the morning frost chewed.

Forgiveness is a star above a frozen lake,
and fires along the shore still warm
the hands that struck you toward the ice.

When you throw your bread into the sea,
walk away and do not pitch your tent
until the high-peak snows rise at your back.

Every friend lies like an open land
full of promise, but summer comes,
and the fall, and the interminable age of ice.

Do not ask for tenderness; learn to snarl.
And when the dawn's frost comes, turn
and rage at the darkness for it's passing.

II. Prayer muttered into morning

Least of all the human, hardly the bear,
perhaps the toad—who comes nearest dying
loves most honestly the cracking river floe.

A long return from the forest through snow,
weariness to the legs, a harrowing of the heart,
brings wood to the cold fires along the shore.

The clasp of ungloved hands in winter air
and the shared chattering of teeth by a rising fire

are prayer muttered into morning.

"I tell of land with broad rivers and long sun"
is story for the old to give the young, shivering
under blankets, crouching around early fires.

A human stands to the knees in snow,
watching the sun lift its flame to the peaks,
asking, "How can I go down to the shore?"

Waving Man, 5th Street and I-35, Waco

Every new day we saw him, old
seer of our sunrise, minister of morning.

Flailing oracle, thundering his orations,
the waving man still dances frantic,
wild between relentless traffic lanes,
flinging down his weird word-hoard
against the frenetic monotone of wheels.
Lone denizen of a diminished Eden,
he presses along the margins of highway,
homeless in his squeezed field of grass
littered with flung bottles and bags—

This Adam attenuate at sunrise rises,
dew-covered, and pumps his arm,
his outstretched palm welcoming,
conferring his bounty of blessings,
or his solitary finger signaling an edict
of disgust-become-indifference,
or his fire-and-sulfur fist
pounding the proclamations of God
against our startled faces.

Lunatic jester, exile of mental ward,
come sing your fierce-weird songs
into my waking dreams; awaken me,
or I may die in my walking sleep.
Oh desperate man blacker than coffee
and pungent with the sweat of zeal,
holler and howl to me my matins.
Punch and puff and guffaw through
the near absolute white noise of the world.

The Day Becomes Cathedral

How we neglect our chances,
waiting instead for church,
measuring the meantime by dollars
and dollars by the height of rooftops.

These should be occasion enough—
the antiphonal light of a high gable,
a small porch like a pulpit,
a bird bath as baptismal,
the sparrow-choirs gorgeous
in their burnished browns.

What day, what rain-soaked
fog-shrouded day, does not become
cathedral, does not discover
some convenient place for awe,
even a dank grotto beneath trees?

Marvel as well from the shade
of a sun-fired bush or from
the surface of a wet black stone.

Hunger Drives the Crescent Swallow's Wings

This far inland, gulls
dance behind chisels and plows,
dive and squall among furrows.
Their cries do not reach
for the gray green horizons
of the earth's curve.

With undulant shoulders,
geese came in waves last night.
Despite their raptured calls,
they bent their wings in hunger,
not for lavendar of sunset
or vermilion of sunrise.

A blue heron holds
a bluegill in the rapiers of her bill.
She and the doomed fish answer,
not the composition of cattails
and water in blues and browns,
but the pull of her craw.

Near the banks, a watcher
stands, still as windless reeds,
keen to a slow advance of shadows,
while through the arcs and attitudes
of flight, hunger drives the crescent
swallow's wings.

Watching Eastward

She would not hear of westward trains
and of mothers in the same conversation.

She set her biscuits, cups, and saucers
in meticulous order, like a little girl--
one for herself, one for her mother.

When the train came, like trains do,
howling and thundering
with the ritual rhythm of wheels
and rails and exhaust billowing,

she kept her tea cup poised, until
the engine blew her to smithereens.

Her tea set stays in the cupboard now,
yet see how agile the dying can be,
how like athletes they may leap aboard:

The mother, her tea parties done,
boarded the westward train, smiling,
and with a stern look and a look of pity
for the daughter left at home in disarray.

Fossil

Here is a riverbed, familiar, and dry now for years.
The dryness too is familiar.

It is marked off from the desert only by the rough banks
where sleek fish no longer hide.

I stand in it, among stones and the stubble of willows,
turning a fossil over in my hands—

A breeze moans among rocks, or a deep-throated bird
calls from the shade of a cactus—

It is your voice, coming suddenly, without reason, cruelly
as friends' voices do when friends have gone—

And I touch the impress, the intricate, detailed body
of your absence.

Made in the USA
Middletown, DE
04 January 2017